D0966155

THE WISDOM

of the

TIBETAN LAMAS

TIMOTHY FREKE

JE

First published in 1998 by Journey Editions, an imprint of
Periplus Editions (HK) Ltd., with editorial offices at
153 Milk Street, Boston, Massachusetts 02109.

Distributed by:
USA
Charles E. Tuttle Co., Inc. RR 1 Box 231-5
North Clarendon, VT 05759
Tel.: (802) 773-8930 Fax.: (802) 773-6993

Japan
Tuttle Shokai Ltd. 1-21-13, Seki
Tama-ku, Kawasaki-shi
Kanagawa-ken 214
Japan
Tel.: (044) 833-0225 Fax.: (044) 822-0413

Southeast Asia
Berkeley Books Pte. Ltd. 5 Little Road #08-01
Singapore 536983
Tel.: (65) 280-3320 Fax.: (65) 280-6290

ISBN 1-885203-58-6
The Catalog Card Number is on file with
the Library of Congress

Printed in Hong Kong

CONTENTS

Introduction

Buddhism was inspired by a 6th-century-BC enlightened master from India, known by the title of Buddha. He taught that it is possible for each one of us to awaken our immortal and permanent essential nature, and so end the suffering caused by the impermanence of this shifting world. Buddhism developed into two different schools known as Theravada and Mahayana. The Mahayana or "Greater Vehicle" school of Buddhism spread to Tibet briefly in the late 8th century AD, and then more steadily from the 13th century AD. An important strand of Buddhism that has particularly

flourished in Tibet is Tantric Buddhism, that stems from Indian yoga techniques that encourage spiritual transformation.

The Tibetan word for Buddhist is "nangpa" which means "insider." Tibetan Buddhism is about looking inside to discover the essential nature of the mind. The outer world is an illusion. The underlying reality is what the Tibetan Book of the Dead calls the "Clear Light of the Void" – Consciousness itself. A direct awareness of this as our true immortal nature is enlightenment.

Tibetan culture is completely dominated by Buddhism. Its temporal leader as well as its spiritual leader is His Holiness the Dalai Lama. "Lama" means teacher. The Dalai Lama is a "Bodhisattva" or "Wisdom-Being" – spiritual master who reincarnates over and over again out of compassion, to help all sentient beings reach enlightenment and end their suffering. Tibetan Buddhism is far more than veneration for a Buddha who lived 2,500 years ago. It has been inspired and shaped by a succession of living Buddhas, who embody the potential within us all to experience spiritual liberation. It is a path open to all of us, regardless of how imperfect we currently feel. One of the most famous Buddhist masters, Milarepa, was formerly a murderer, yet in the same lifetime achieved enlightenment.

1 The Clear Light of Consciousness

All suffering comes from believing ourselves to be what we are not. We think we are a body and personality that is born to die, but our true identity is unborn and so never dying. We are the Mind of the universe. The separate ego-self is a phantom with no essential reality. There are no separate individual entities at all, because all things are so intimately interrelated that nothing has any independent existence. Enlightenment is the awareness of pure Consciousness that contains the appearance of separate things, but which is in itself a Oneness empty of all separateness.

Buddhahood cannot be found outside,
but only by contemplating the
nature of your mind.

MILAREPA

"It is your own awareness right now.
It is simple, natural, and clear.
Why say "I don't understand what the mind is?"
There is nothing to think about,
just permanent clear Consciousness.
Why say "I don't see the reality of the mind?"
The mind is the thinker of these thoughts.
Why say "When I look I can't find it?"
No looking is necessary.
Why say "Whatever I try doesn't work?"
It is enough to remain simple.
Why say "How can I do nothing?"
It is good to be a non-doer.
Why say "I can't achieve this?"
The void of pure Consciousness is naturally present.
Why say "Spiritual practice doesn't reveal it?"
It is spontaneous and free from cause and effect.
Why say "The search is futile?"
Thought and liberation exist simultaneously.
Why say "All medicines are impotent?"
This awareness is the medicine.
Why say "I don't know?""

PADMA SAMBHAVA

One Mind pervading all life.
It is the primal state, that goes unnoticed.
It is brilliant, boundless intelligence,
that is ignored.
It appears everywhere and always,
but is not seen.

PADMA SAMBHAVA

“Astounding! The self-creating Clear Light has always been!
Astounding! It is parentless pure Consciousness!
Astounding! Primal wisdom has no creator!
Astounding! It has never known birth and could never die!
Astounding! It is obvious everywhere,
but with no one there to see it!
Astounding! It has been lost in illusion,
but no harm has touched it!
Astounding! It is enlightenment itself,
yet no good has come to it!
Astounding! It exists in everyone, but has been overlooked!
Astounding! Yet we go on looking for something other!
Astounding! It is the only thing that is ours
yet we look for it elsewhere!
Astounding! Astounding!”

PADMA SAMBHAVA

Through perfect seeing all discrimination is dissolved into a non-conceptual state.

MILAREPA

The true nature of things is void, spacious and naked as the sky. The clear light of emptiness, without a center or a circumference, is the dawning of the awareness of pure Consciousness.

TIBETAN BOOK OF THE DEAD

Know that all appearances are like a dream; illusionary projections of your mind. Grasping nothing, beyond all concepts, rest in the wisdom of pure Consciousness.

TSELE NATSOK RANGDROL

Just as undisturbed water is clear and transparent, so an undisturbed mind is naturally blissful.

TIBETAN SAYING

"You are like a poor man who doesn't realize
he lives on top of buried treasure.
The earth of body, mind, and speech
obscures the fact that you are already
enlightened and keeps you impoverished
by the sufferings of life."

KUNKYEN LONGCHEN RABJAM

You don't have to do anything with your mind,
just let it naturally rest in its essential nature.
Your own mind, unagitated, is Reality.
Meditate on this without distraction.
Know the Truth beyond all opposites.
Thoughts are like bubbles
that form and dissolve in clear water.
Thoughts are not distinct from the absolute Reality,
so relax, there's no need to be critical.
Whatever arises, whatever occurs,
simply don't cling to it, but immediately let it go.
What you see, hear, and touch are your own mind.
There is nothing but mind.
Mind transcends birth and death.
The essence of mind is pure Consciousness,
that never leaves Reality;
even though it experiences the things of the senses.
In the equanimity of the Absolute,
there is nothing to renounce or attain.

NIGUMA

“ One thing is made up of many parts
and in itself does not exist.
There is nothing that is not made up of many parts.
Without the idea of “one thing”
the many does not exist,
and without the idea of existence
there is no non-existence. ”

NAGARJUNA

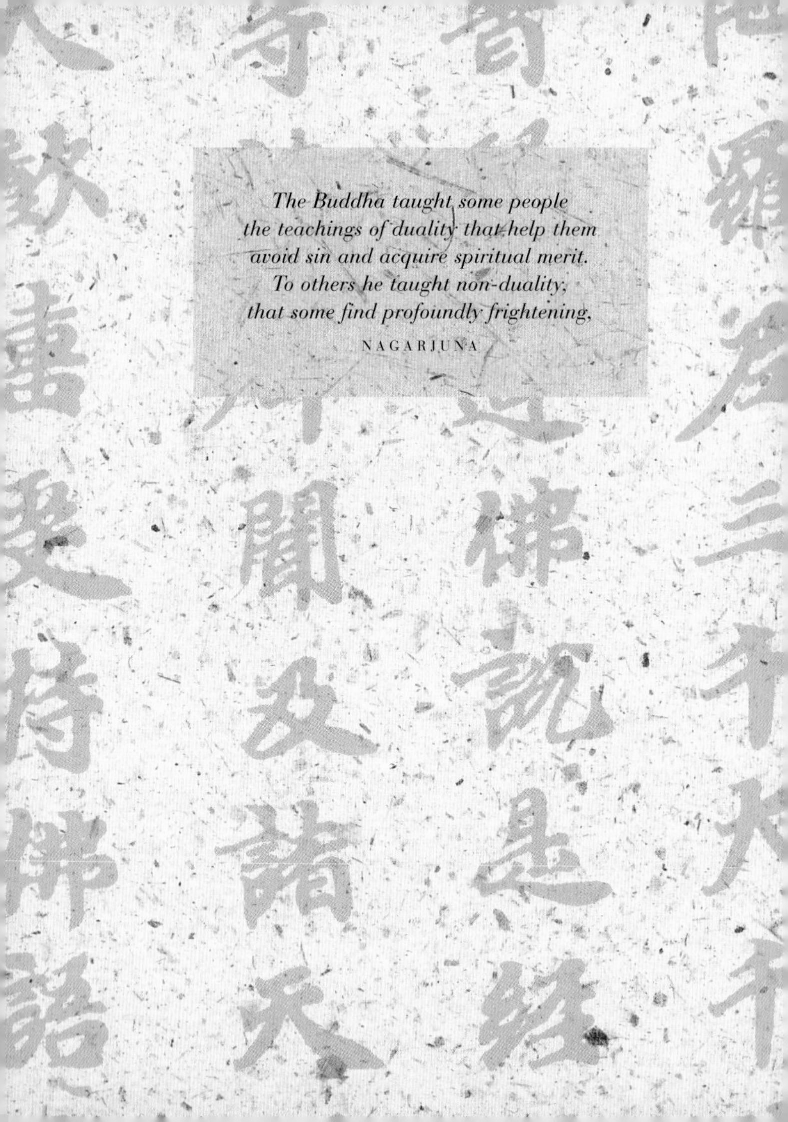

The Buddha taught some people
the teachings of duality that help them
avoid sin and acquire spiritual merit.
To others he taught non-duality,
that some find profoundly frightening,

NAGARJUNA

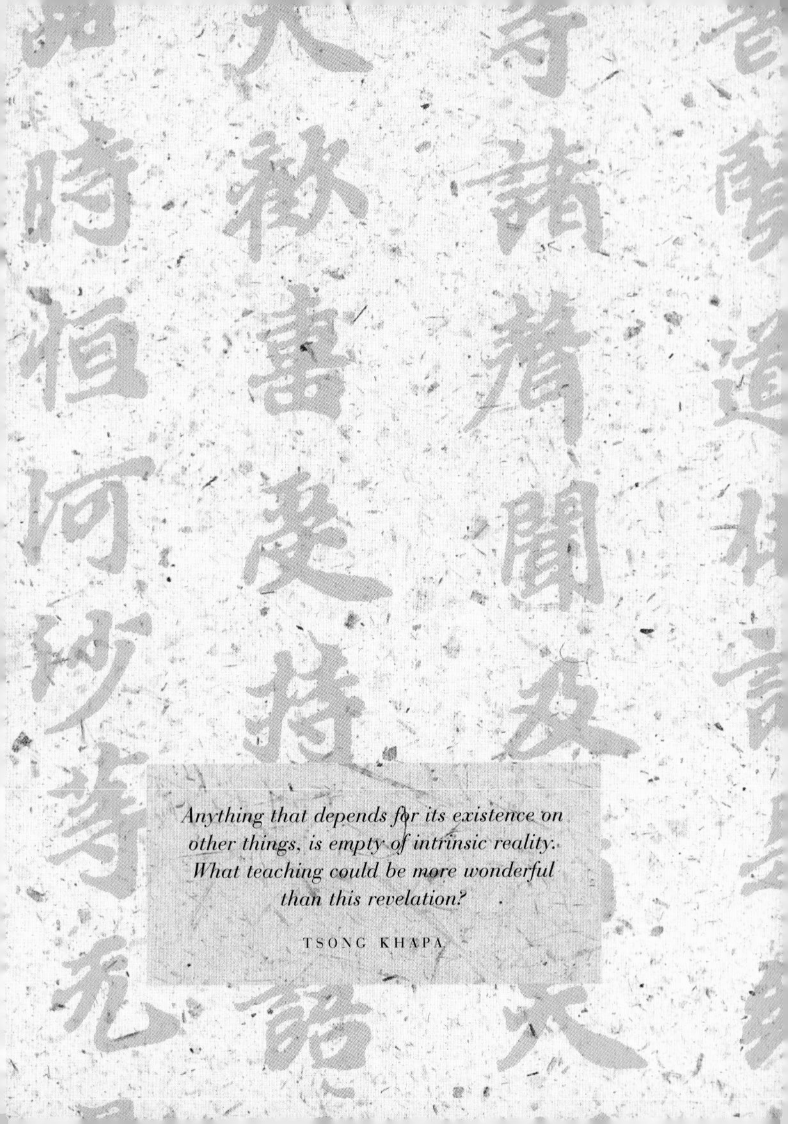

Anything that depends for its existence on other things, is empty of intrinsic reality. What teaching could be more wonderful than this revelation?

TSONG KHAPA

Like it or not,
if you look at your own mind you will
discover it is void and groundless;
as insubstantial as empty space.

PADMA SAMBHAVA

Our Physical and psychological identity
arises from the false idea of an "I." It
grows from an illusionary seed, so how
could it possibly be real? Just as you can't
see your own face only a reflection in a
mirror, so the "I" does not exist apart
from your illusionary identity.

NAGARJUNA

Through the power of habit
I have come to view an insignificant
sperm and egg as myself.

SHANTIDEVA

"The Buddha asked Subhuti, "Does one who has immersed himself in the stream that flows to enlightenment say of himself 'I have entered the stream'?" Subhuti replied, "No, Buddha. He is called a stream-enterer because he knows he has attained nothing. If the thought 'I have attained the state of entering the stream' were to occur to him, then he would be clutching to a personality or soul or some idea of a separate self."

Subhuti asked the Buddha, "In distant future times of darkness will there be those who believe these truths?" The Buddha replied, "There will never be beings to believe these truths, for I have taught you that although we speak of 'beings' there are actually no separate entities.""

DIAMOND SUTRA

“The mountains are a joyous place full of flowers.
Monkeys play in the forest trees.
Songbirds sing and insects swarm.
A rainbow shines both day and night.
Summer and winter bring soothing rain.
Spring and autumn bring shifting fog.
Solitary, in simple clothes, I am happy here
because I see the Clear Light
and contemplate the emptiness.
I am delighted by appearances
because my body is free from bad actions.
A strong mind wanders contentedly
and is naturally cheerful.”

MILAREPA

*“I am not, nor will I be. I have nothing,
nor will I have.”
This frightens the immature
but dispels all fear in the wise.*

NAGARJUNA

11 The Compassionate Bodhisattva

Enlightenment is an experience of the fundamental nature of mind, that is all-loving. A Bodhisattva is a master who sees that in reality there are no separate beings, yet is moved by this insight to feel deep compassion for all those who are still suffering from the delusion of separateness. Having overcome their sense of being a separate self, Bodhisattvas devote themselves to selfless service. They take a solemn vow to forgo complete liberation from the cycle of death and rebirth to reincarnate over and over again in order that they may help all sentient beings become enlightened.

> "Others are my main concern.
> When I notice something of mine,
> I steal it and give it to others."
>
> SHANTIDEVA

The one thing to be attained is essentially void and compassionate. Let me explain. The realization of voidness is the absolute spirit of enlightenment; it is seeing that all things are unborn. Compassion is the relative spirit of enlightenment; it is reaching out in love to all beings who have yet to realize that they are unborn. Those who follow the Mahayana path should develop these two forms of the spirit of enlightenment.

DROM

The supreme goal of the teachings is the emptiness whose essence is compassion.

ATISHA

My religion is kindness.
HIS HOLINESS
THE DALAI LAMA

“An aged lama practiced meditation by a small pond. But no sooner had he crossed his legs and began his prayers then he would notice a little insect drowning in the water and get up to rescue it. Every day was the same, until his fellow monks became concerned that he was never actually practicing any meditation. They suggested he chose another spot where he would be undisturbed or that he meditate with his eyes closed so that he would not see the little insects in the water. Then he would achieve enlightenment more quickly and be in position to truly help all sentient beings. The aged lama thanked his brothers for their concern but replied, "How can a worthless old man like me, who has taken a vow to devote this life and all subsequent lives to rescuing sentient beings, sit with closed eyes and a closed heart meditating on compassion while these helpless insects are suffering before me?"”

TIBETAN TEACHING STORY

Know emptiness,
be compassionate.

MILAREPA

Even offering three hundred bowls of food three times a day does not match the spiritual merit gain in one moment of love.

NAGARJUNA

All meditation must begin with arousing deep compassion. Whatever one does must emerge from an attitude of love and benefiting others.

MILAREPA

All happiness comes from the desire for others to be happy.
All misery comes form the desire for oneself to be happy.

SHANTIDEVA

"If I give what's in it for me?"
This is the selfish way of demon's.
"If I receive what can I give?"
This the selfless way of the gods.

SHANTIDEVA

Just as habit creates a sense of self in this body that is completely without a self, why can't we habitually extend that sense of self to all beings?

SHANTIDEVA

If you are attached to
your own interests,
you don't have the mind
of the enlightened.

GÜNPA NYINGPO

All beings are my relations.
Life is beginningless and
so are my rebirths.
Passing through innumerable lives
I have taken on every form countless times
and inhabited every country.
There is not one being who has not been
my mother many times and will be many
more times in the future.

MAITREYA'S TEACHINGS TO ASANGA

“ We view the hand as a limb of the body with no separate existence, so why don't we view all beings as limbs of the body of Life? I'm not proud of being altruistic. I don't expect a reward for feeding myself. ”

SHANTIDEVA

As long as space exits
and sentient beings endure,
may I also remain
to dispel the misery of the world.

SHANTIDEVA

“ When you and I are alike in both
desiring happiness,
what is so special about me that I care
about myself only?

When you and I are alike in both not
desiring pain, what's so special about
me, that I don't care for you equally? ”

SHANTIDEVA

"Subhuti asked the Buddha, "How does one walk the Bodhisattva path?" Buddha answered, "When traveling the Bodhisattva path one should always think 'I will bring all beings to enlightenment, yet even when this is accomplished, in reality, no beings have been brought to enlightenment.' If the idea of a personality or separate self should ever arise, he is not a Bodhisattva."

The Buddha said to Subhuti, "Never imagine that one who has arrived thinks to himself 'I have liberated others;' for there is no one to be liberated. If a Buddha thought he had liberated someone he would have the concept of a personality or separate self."

Subhuti asked the Buddha, "In the future will there be any beings who understand the truth of these teachings?" The Buddha answered, "Even in the distant future there will be good and wise Bodhisattvas who understand. Such Bodhisattvas will not honor or root themselves in only one Buddha, but will place themselves under countless Buddhas. Why is this, Subhuti? Because these Bodhisattvas will have no notion of a personality, or an ego, or a separate self.""

DIAMOND SUTRA

“Bodhisattvas see all beings like parents see their only son. They are delighted to see him practicing goodness, but when their son is ill they are filled with empathy and are constantly concerned. Likewise when Bodhisattvas see any being enmeshed in the illness of illusion, their hearts ache with compassion.

When a child puts dirty things into his mouth, his parents are worried that he will hurt himself and remove the item. Likewise when Bodhisattvas see beings who are not mature acting misguidedly in body, speech, and mind, they use the hand of wisdom to save them from their mistakes, because they do not wish that they repeat birth and death, and so receive more suffering and anxiety.”

MAHAPARINIRVANA SUTRA

May no sentient beings, even insects,
be bound to the illusion of life.
May I be empowered to save them all.

MILAREPA

I am always near to those with faith,
and even those without faith,
although they do not know it.
I will never cease to protect my children
with my unending compassion

PADMA SAMBHAVA

The immature work
to benefit themselves.
Buddhas work to benefit others.
Look at the difference
between these two.
What more can I say?

SHANTIDEVA

"May I be a protector to the vulnerable;
a guide to those traveling;
a bridge to those pining
for the farther shore.
May the suffering of all completely cease.
May I be the healer and the medicine,
nursing all the sick of this world,
until everyone is well."

SHANTIDEVA

III The Dharma

Enlightenment is the realization that the separate self is in reality an illusion. The path to enlightenment is the purification of all selfishness through cultivating goodness and eradicating harmful thoughts, words, and deeds. This is known as the Dharma or Buddhist Way. The Buddha is said to have taught 84,000 different methods to pacify negative emotions such as anger, blame, hate, and greed. However, all teachings must ultimately be put aside. Enlightenment is beyond all ideas and practices. It is not about acting or thinking in certain ways, it is simply being what we actually are.

A bright light in a vase illuminates nothing.
Likewise the essential Truth shines within
but is blocked and prevented. Break the
obscuring vase, however, and the light will
naturally shine everywhere.

KUNKYEN LONGCHEN RABJAM

“If the teachings are not understood the idea of "I" remains.
Then comes the concepts of good and bad actions
leading to better or worse rebirths.

As long as the teaching that destroys
the misconception of "I" is not understood,
always carefully practice generosity, morality, and patience.”

PADMA SAMBHAVA

“Ignorant acts are the pointless cause
of all misery, completely unhelpful now
and at the moment of death.
Pluck them out like irritating thorns.”

KUNKYEN LONGCHEN RABJAM

“The 12th century master Geshe Ben was renown for his goodness and integrity. Once, while begging for alms, a family of devout Buddhists invited him to their home to be fed. He was so hungry that he found it difficult to wait while his hosts were elsewhere preparing the meal. To his complete shock he found himself stealing food from a jar when no one was looking. Geshe Ben suddenly burst into loud cries of “Thief! Thief! I've caught you red-handed.” His hosts rushed into the room to find him berating himself and threatening his hand with being cut off if it ever behaved like that again.”

TIBETAN TEACHING STORY

If one hides the evil, it multiplies and grows.
If one bares it and repents, the sin dies out.
Therefore all Buddhas say
that the wise do not hide sin.

MAHAPARINIRVANA SUTRA

Don't overlook small and seemingly insignificant negative actions. The smallest of sparks can burn down a mountain.

TIBETAN SAYING

It is natural for the immature to harm others. Getting angry with them is like resenting a fire for burning.

SHANTIDEVA

Compassionate One! I confess and solemnly vow never to repeat all sinful acts that I have committed or took pleasure in other's committing, from the beginning of time.

PANCHEN LAMA I,
LOSANG CHÖKYI GYALTSEN

If someone beats you with a stick it is the stick-not the assailant that hurts you, so why get angry with the attacker? The attacker is just a puppet of hate anyway, so get angry only with hate.

SHANTIDEVA

“Goodness creates a joyous and happy life.

Abstain from killing
and you will know a long, healthy lifespan.

Abstain from stealing and you will have supreme wealth.

Abstain from inappropriate sexuality
and you will have a contented marriage.

Abstain from lying
and you will acquire praise and honor.

Abstain from criticism
and you will delight in friendly conversation.

Abstain from slander
and you will enjoy harmonious relationships.

Abstain from gossiping
and others will trust you.

Abstain from greed and your needs will be met.

Abstain from spite and you will be at peace.

Abstain from wrong thinking
and you will be optimistic.

These ten virtues are like a chariot to take you to heaven.”

KUNKYEN LONGCHEN RABJAM

“When I relate to others,
may I see myself as the lesser
and value others as greater.

When I act, may I be mindful of habitual reactions,
and prevent them harming myself and others.

When I meet an evil person possessed
by suffering and error,
may I value them as if I have happened
upon a treasure chest.

When some jealously attacks me without cause,
may I let them be the winner
and willingly embrace defeat.

When someone I trust unreasonably harms me,
may I see them as my greatest spiritual guide.”

GESHE LANGRI TANGPA DORJEY SENGEY

All philosophies
are mental fabrications.
There has never been a single
doctrine by which one could enter
the true essence of things.

NAGARJUNA

Whatever happens, I will not let my
cheerfulness be disturbed.
Being unhappy won't get me anywhere
and will dissipate all my goodness.
Why be unhappy about something if you
can change it? And if you can't,
how will being unhappy help?

SHANTIDEVA

Those who are too clever,
completely miss the point.

TIBETAN SAYING

“The greatest achievement is selflessness.
The greatest worth is self-mastery.
The greatest quality is seeking to serve others.
The greatest precept is continual awareness.
The greatest medicine is the emptiness of everything.
The greatest action is not conforming with the world's ways.
The greatest magic is transmuting the passions.
The greatest generosity is non-attachment.
The greatest goodness is a peaceful mind.
The greatest patience is humility.
The greatest effort is not concerned with results.
The greatest meditation is a mind that lets go.
The greatest wisdom is seeing through appearances.”

ATISHA

“Rely on the truth the teacher teaches,
not on his personality.
Rely on what he means,
not on the words he speaks.
Rely on the real meaning,
not a partial provisional understanding.
Rely on your wisdom mind,
not on the judgmental intellect.”

THE FOUR RELIANCES
TAUGHT BY THE BUDDHA

Speak the truth.
Speak kindly.
Speak what is pleasant.
Speak what is helpful.
Speak what is needed.
Speak with intention.
Speak without criticism.
Speak independently.
Speak well.

NAGARJUNA

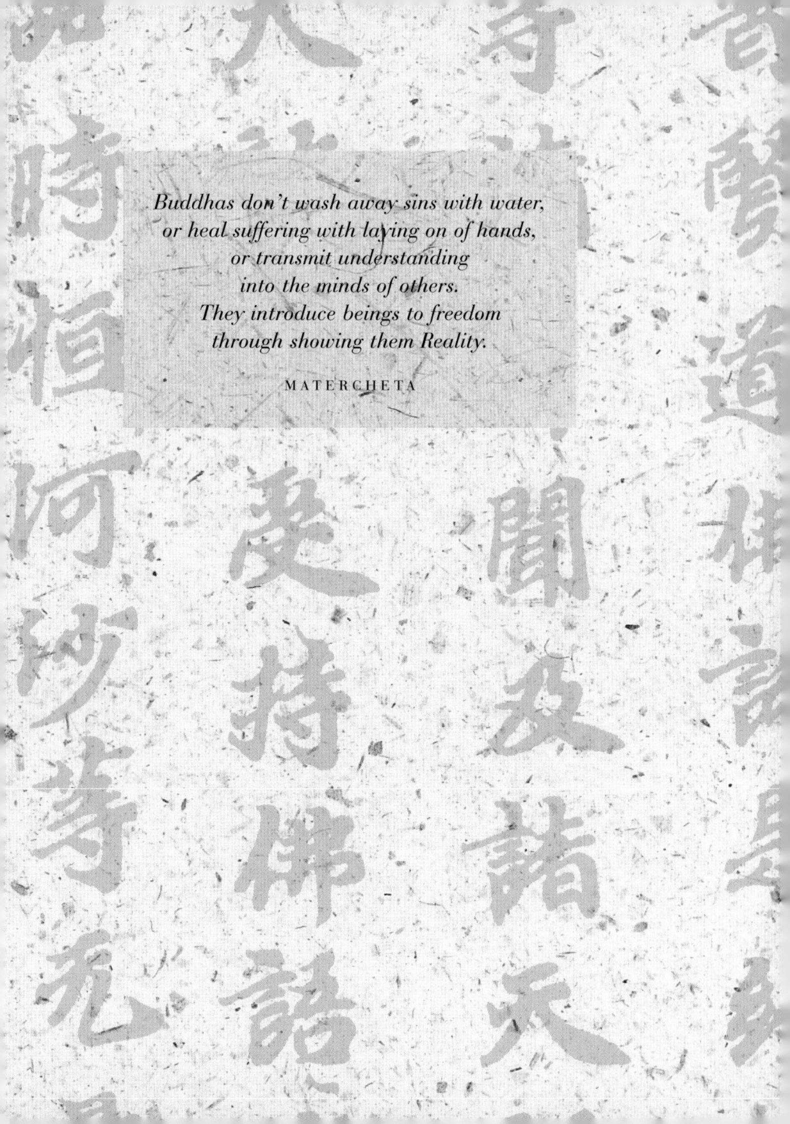

Buddhas don't wash away sins with water,
or heal suffering with laying on of hands,
or transmit understanding
into the minds of others.
They introduce beings to freedom
through showing them Reality.

MATERCHETA

If you hold to a particular perspective,
you don't have the correct perspective.

GÜNPA NYINGPO

Even a desire for more instruction is a
distraction. Too many explanations
without the essence is like an orchard
of trees without fruit. Knowing many
explanations is not knowing the Truth.
Too much conceptualisation has no
spiritual benefit. Only the secret
treasure benefits the heart.
If you want riches, concentrate on this.

MILAREPA

Don't mistake understanding
for realization.
Don't mistake realization
for liberation.

TIBETAN SAYING

" Milarepa was Gampopa's master for many years.
Just before Milarepa died Gampopa asked him
for some final instructions. Milarepa replied
"What is required is more effort, not more teachings."
As Gampopa departed, knowing that he would not
see his master again, Milarepa shouted after him
"There is one profound secret that I would not show
to just anyone." Gampopa looked back toward his master.
Milarepa turned, bent over, and pulling up his old robes
revealed the huge callouses that covered his buttocks,
the results of many years of meditation sat
on hard rough rocks. "My beloved son," said the master
"this is my final instruction." "

TIBETAN TEACHING STORY

"Coming across a monk praying while circumambulating a holy building, Geshe Tenpa said, "How pleasant to walk around sacred places, but you know its far better to practice the wonderful Dharma." The monk took his words to heart and began earnestly studying the scriptures. One day Geshe Tenpa came across him and commented, "How commendable it is to study the scriptures, but you know it is far better to practice the wonderful Dharma." The monk took his words to heart and took up intensive meditation. One day Geshe Tenpa came across him and said, "How blissful to be lost in one-pointed meditation, but you know it is far better to practice the wonderful Dharma." The monk was completely confounded. In desperation he begged, "Master, teach me what to do." Geshe Tenpa smiled and replied, "Just give up grasping at things.""

TIBETAN TEACHING STORY

The precepts of the living lama
are more important than the scriptures.

ATISHA

IV Death

A human life is a great blessing achieved after innumerable lives evolving through other forms. It is a precious opportunity to spiritually awaken, that we should fully embrace. The Tibetan Book of the Dead, a sort of guide book to the realms after death, teaches that when we die we will all experience for ourselves the Clear Light of Consciousness. If we have used our lives to spiritually awaken, we will recognize it as our own essential nature and so become free from the cycle of death and rebirth. If not, we will spend some time in a heaven or hell before reincarnating.

> “Strong and healthy, who thinks of sickness
> until it strikes like lightening?
>
> Preoccupied with the world, who thinks of death,
> until it arrives like thunder?”
>
> MILAREPA

" With your heart contemplate the certainty that all your relations and all your wealth will be as nothing, like a deserted city. Everything is impermanent, so be detached.

With your heart contemplate the inevitability of death. When it comes, your home and possessions, your friends and famous colleagues, will not accompany you. Realize the absolute Truth. "

KUNKYEN LONGCHEN RABJAM

That "corpse" you dread
so much is living with you
right here and now!

MILAREPA

Imagine an ox's yoke adrift
on the vast ocean and a turtle
happening to poke its head
though the hole –
this is how rare
and extraordinary it is to
be born a human being.

KUNKYEN LONGCHEN RABJAM

Humans prepare
for the future all their lives,
yet meet the next life
totally unprepared.

DRAKPA GYALTSEN

" O nobly-born, the time has now come for you to seek the way in reality. Your breathing is about to cease. Your guru has previously set you face to face with the Clear Light; and now you are about to experience it in its Reality in the after-death state, in which all things are like the void and cloudless sky, and naked, pure Consciousness is like a transparent vacuum without circumference or center. At this moment, know your Self and stay in that state. I, too, at this time, am setting you face to face.

O nobly-born, listen. Now you are experiencing the Radiance of the Clear Light of Pure Reality. Recognize it. O nobly-born, your present mind, in essence naturally empty and without characteristics is Reality. Your own mind is the void; yet it is not nothingness but Consciousness itself. Unobstructed, shining, thrilling, and blissful, it is the all-good Buddha. Your own mind, void and inseparable from the Great Body of Radiance, knows neither birth nor death. It is the Immutable Light-Buddha.

This knowledge is sufficient. Recognize the voidness of your own mind to be Buddhahood. To be conscious of Consciousness is to keep yourself in the state of the Buddha-Mind. "

TIBETAN BOOK OF THE DEAD

Soon you will inevitably die,
and nothing will be of any assistance.
The experience of death
is simply your own thoughts.
Don't concoct illusions,
but let them all dissolve
into the vast awareness
of Consciousness itself.

TSELE NATSOK RANGDROL

“My delight in death
exceeds the pleasure of a merchant
who makes a vast fortune,
or a victorious war god,
or a sage in total trance.
Like a traveller taking to the road,
I will leave this world and return home
to the limitless bliss of deathlessness.
My life is over and my karma is done with.
The benefit from praying is exhausted.
Things of the world are abandoned.
The show is over.
In the pure after-death states
I will instantly realize the essence of my being.
I am approaching the ground of primal perfection.”

LONGCHENPA

All beings have lived and died innumerable times, and have known the ineffable Clear Light, but because they are lost in the darkness of ignorance they wander in the never ending illusion.

PADMA SAMBHAVA

The publishers would like to thank the following for the use of pictures:

Brian Beresford: pp. 35, 37, 46
e.t. archive: pp. 4, 9, 59
Vanessa Fletcher: pp. 5, 8, 13, 19, 27, 28, 32, 39, 40, 41, 44, 51, 52, 55, 57
Tibet Images: pp. 15, 25
Tibet Image Bank: p. 18